PU
Awaken   Succeed?

Elvira Guzman

Published by Arivle Media Group

To order additional copies of this book, or to book the

author to lecture on the book, contact us at

Madelyn@elviegpr.com or visit www.elviraguzman.com

Published in Covina, California by Arivle Media Group.

This book may be purchased in bulk for educational,

business, fund-raising, or sales promotional use. For

information, please email us.

Printed in the United States

Dedication

This book is dedicated to everyone who feels lost and wants to find their purpose. This book was created just for you, so you can begin to enjoy your journey now!

Table of Contents

Preface

It took a sickness that put me on the brink of death to finally reflect on my life and my purpose. All my life, I have been working, busy since age 14, when my parents were incarcerated and I was left to fend for myself. In college, I worked for celebrity Steve Harvey, and honed my business acumen to start my own publicity firm, Elvie G PR. For years, I poured my energy and efforts into my work, until I realized it was literally killing me. Since then, I have worked towards discovering and acting on my true purpose, which is to help others. This book is one of the ways I seek to help others to awaken. To reach out to me and get additional support on discovering your purpose, please visit my website, www.elviraguzman.com

Foreword

By Troy Byer

Once in a while, we have the good fortune of meeting individuals we hope to know for a lifetime. The universe was clearly conspiring on my behalf the day I met Elvira, and I was thrilled when she agreed to help me promote my heart work as my publicist. In a short matter of time, I realized that Elvira being my publicist was merely the reason why we met. Through many seasons, years and over a decade later my relationship with Elvira continues to evolve and thrive in various domains. In addition to being a great publicist, Elvira is someone I can authentically call a friend.

It has been a pure pleasure witnessing Elvira's growth and development over the years. And anyone who knows Elvira also knows that second to her profound love for God is her unwavering commitment to making a difference in the lives of others. In this book, Elvira offers her readers a wealth of information and tools designed to do exactly that – make a difference. Pulling powerfully from her past experiences, relationships, and life lessons, Elvira brings forth a wisdom that surpasses her age and yet, remains relatable and applicable to all of us regardless of our age. Elvira's unbridled compassion and empathy for humanity crescendos with each turn of the page.

If you are looking for your purpose in life, this book will help you find it. Understanding the importance of digging where we stumble, Elvira does an excellent job demonstrating how it is that our pain can serve as our purpose compass. For those of us inflicted with the experience of being victimized in life, Elvira lovingly offers insight and access to dismantling that false reality too.

In this book, Elvira dives deep into the power of thought, the magic of clarity, the possibilities available for those of us who have a plan. She also powerfully demonstrates the importance of self-love and the necessity of forgiveness. Without a doubt, Elvira leaves no stone unturned as her words lovingly awaken us to new horizons, confirming God's promise that we truly can have as far as we can see. In your hands, you hold a book created by an individual who actually understands that being a leader is measured by the number of leaders created, not by the number of followers baited. Elvira is a true leader who journeyed fearlessly into the crevices of her heart, mind, body and soul to write this book. May her lessons serve as gifts for us all as her teachings on these pages unfold.

Introduction

*"God created each of us with a special gift that we must use
to help others. That special gift is our purpose"*

We are all purpose-driven people and children of God. He
sends us here to achieve a Purpose for the betterment of the world.
When we are not busy working on that we are here to enjoy life!

One person's purpose may be to discover the cure for
cancer, and another may be to spread the message of love. It varies!
The harder the purpose, the tougher the life, because you will
inevitably gain strength, confidence, and resilience with each
obstacle. And each obstacle attracts new people to your journey
towards your purpose. It is extremely important that we know
exactly who we are. At our core, we are all children of the Divine
and we all experience pain, joy, disappointment, love, and obstacles
to build our strength.

God created each of us with a special gift that we must use
to help others. That special gift is our purpose. When we don't
follow our life's purpose, God sends us signs to let us know we

must get back on track. A great example is: if you are a truck driver and God's purpose for you is to be a preacher, God will send you obstacle after obstacle so you change jobs and fulfill your purpose.

Love is the same way. If we are not supposed to be with someone, God will send us signs and hints to move us away, and towards the person we truly belong with.

In the game of life, we are all players, and God is our coach. When a life trauma happens, like the loss of a parent, a car accident, a divorce, or near-death experience, God must substitute in a stronger player to survive in our shell, even if we have to skip a phase. This explains why you sometimes meet a 7-year-old girl who talks and acts like a 15-year-old. The child had to overcome tough obstacles, and to ensure her survival, God has made her more mature, knowledgeable, and wise than most children her age.

The silver lining in being forced to grow up too soon is that those kids often become very successful adults. They had to start working, hustling, and figuring out life before their peers. They have a head start on the rest of the players in this game.

Take the play-by-play of my life, for example. I was only 14 when my parents were sent to jail. As a teenager, I had to transition to an adult. Instead of worrying about boys and school, my focus shifted to worrying about work and bills. Suddenly, I was a 35-year-old woman in a 14-year-old girl's body because I had so many responsibilities and no time. I didn't get to truly enjoy high school or college.

However, now I am able to go to high schools and speak about my experiences I have lectured at colleges like USC. In this way, I am able to enjoy and spend time in those places again. In addition, I also find time now to do things I wish I had time to do growing up, like painting or hiking. Years later, I am finally catching up on all the things I had missed. Life is about perspective, and I choose to think positive. I've had the ability to work for some of the wealthiest and most famous people in the U.S. and through their mentorship I've read a lot of books and I've gained wisdom.

My deepest desire is to share with you the knowledge I've gained so that you too can be truly successful! In doing research I found the most important thing you can do if you want to be happy and successful is to find your purpose in life. Without knowing that you will never attain major success and you will not feel true happiness. You will always feel like something's missing or something is wrong. It's only when you find your purpose in life and start to actively pursue it that you attract all of your blessings to you.

Every person has a purpose and it's up to us to dig deep and find it so that we can fully awaken and be of service to our creator. I truly hope you enjoy this book that was written with so much love.

Chapter 1

Purpose

"God had a plan in mind when God created us"

Let's start by talking PURPOSE! What is Purpose? Everyone seems to be talking about it. The answer is simple: Your purpose is the reason God sent you here. It's the one thing you do that lights your heart on fire. When you're doing it, time flies and outside noises don't distract you because you're so in your zone. That's how you know you are doing something that is associated with your purpose. It just feels right!

Pain is a great way to find purpose. Let's discuss pain. We've all experienced pain, right? It's one of the basic human emotions and none of us will leave this earth without experiencing some form of failure, disappointment, heartbreak, death, accident, mistake, or tragedy. It's inevitable!

Let's do a visual exercise together. Think back to when you experienced extreme pain and ask yourself how did that event/circumstance help you. Many times it makes you stronger, it teaches you how to stand alone, it brings you closer with God and ultimately you start to think with a new perspective.

If you haven't figured out your purpose yet, don't worry. I didn't figure mine out until I was 29. Until then I thought my purpose was to be a publicist and event coordinator until eternity. It wasn't until I became ill and after surgery I had to finally rest and be quiet for a while that I asked myself what makes me happy. There was a time I didn't think I would survive this obstacle and I didn't want to leave this earth without doing what truly made me happy! I realized then joy comes from helping people who are lost find their way back. I was no longer interested in coordinating award shows or chaotic events.

To be honest, I felt in some way I had contributed to my bad health! When I got sick I had just finished doing a big event in Vegas. I didn't eat right, I didn't sleep right, there was a huge turnover within our production team and I had to take responsibility for the entire event. I feel this contributed to my sickness. I had to make an assessment of my life and cut out whatever brought me unnecessary stress. Luckily through rest I was able to reflect on the big questions I never had the time to ask. Sitting here today I thank that obstacle because through that experience I gained my PURPOSE. God always finds a way to redirect us so we may live a purpose driven life... versus a career driven life.

What does religion say about purpose in life:

- The old Testament: "Many are the plans in a person's heart, but it is the Lord's purpose that prevails" (Proverbs 19:21)
- The Quran: "Did you then think that We created you in vain, and that you would not be returned to us?" The Quran 23:115
- Gautama Buddha: "Your purpose in life is to find your purpose and give your whole heart and soul to it"

It's pretty clear based on these teachings; they agree that finding your purpose is the only path to fulfill your plan for God. It's also pretty clear we are to pursue our purpose with all of our heart! God has a plan for us because God wouldn't send us here just to send us here…God had a plan in mind when God created us.

Once I figured out my purpose everything started to make sense. I started to love myself in a way I had never before because instead of being upset with myself for picking the wrong guy or making myself sick, I now knew that everything that had happened to me was not done to me but to guide me closer to my purpose. Some might ask, *"How does my girlfriend leaving me for another guy help me get to my purpose?"*

Simple. Instead of focusing on how it ended, think about what the person brought to your life. Did they introduce you to someone you needed to meet to help with your Purpose? Did they question your job to the point that you finally decided to start your own business? Did you learn lessons from their life that you needed closure in your life? Many people believe relationships are forever, but every relationship will inevitably end through death or divorce. The one relationship that is forever is our relationship with our Creator. Everything else is for a season. Instead of focusing on our pains during our seasons we need to focus on what we gained.

Another outcome of finding my Purpose was my drive to study. I felt I had been focusing on the wrong things all my life and now I wanted to go back and research the things that mattered. Through that research I began to feel a sense of pride because I learned through reading that God is really our parent, not just a figure out there in space with a white beard. For the first time, I realized God really did live in my heart. Yes, when I was young I went to Christian churches and they taught me the song, "I am a C…I am a C-h…I am a C-h-r-i-s-t-i-a-n….and I have C-h-r-is-t in my h-e-a-r-t and I will l-i-v-e -t-e-r-n-a-l-l-y," but I didn't really get it at 4 or 5 years old.

When you know God lives inside you, you start to behave differently. It just happens. If you were a big drinker, you will drink less, or if you eat too much or eat unhealthy foods, you will eat healthy appropriate portions. Something happens in our psyche that wants us to live now, versus just wanting to cope. Alcohol, food, sex, and work are coping mechanisms when you want more and can't find God.

When I found my purpose, interesting things started happening. I stopped eating meat for a long period of time and I took a hiatus from sex. Instead of going out on dates, I found it more interesting to research religion, geography and prophets. I felt an immense hunger for knowledge!

During that time, I wrote my book, *Your Blueprint,* in two days. A gush of energy overcame me. I experienced so much clarity because of my fasting, the book literally burst out of me. Since then, I've dedicated my life to helping others and I've been working with Central Juvenile Hall and at-risk schools throughout Los Angeles to help those who feel lost find their way back.

To further pursue my purpose, I have surrounded myself with people who are actively living a purpose-driven life. Their energy and friendship helps tremendously to stay on the right path. Great friends and family will tell you when you are steering away from your purpose and will keep you focused.

Here are examples of how to find your purpose from pain:

Sexual Abuse Victim –will most likely turn into a School Psychologist or Therapist

- Why: because they wish someone would have stopped what happened to them, so now their mission is to stop the suffering of others
- Major fear: emotional wounds

Physical Abuse Victim- will most likely turn into a Peace Officer/Social Worker

- Why: they seek justice because they feel they didn't have any
- Major fear: physical abuse

Abandoned Child- will most likely turn into an Entrepreneur/Philanthropist

- Why: they will never put their life in someone else's hands
- Major fear: poverty and lack of control

Finding your purpose is important because it's the only thing that will give you complete happiness. Humans have a craving for happiness and we look for it in so many different ways. If we just remember our purpose, most of our toxic behaviors would disappear and we would experience joy again.

Many of you might be thinking, *"So what if I find my purpose in life and then I realize it has nothing to do with my college degree or career?"* Don't worry; shifting from a career-driven life to a purpose-driven life is possible. The shift looks like this:

- Initially 100% all career

- Slowly 75% career with a little purpose work

- Then a 50/50 balance of the two

- Before you know it you are allocating 75% of your energy to your life's purpose

- You are fulfilled, happy and most successful when 100% of your energy is devoted to your purpose

It is never easy to leave what is normal—our career, our major, what society says is normal, what our parents think is dignified—but if we continue to do what others want for us versus what God wants for us, we will continue to be dissatisfied. Buying new cars, purses, houses, changing girlfriends/boyfriends, thinking that will fill that void…the only thing that fills the hole is figuring out why you are here and doing things that achieve that mission.

How You Can Use Your Pain for Purpose

Your obstacles make you stronger because there is a point where you think you will not be able to make it and when you do, you develop tremendous confidence in yourself! This allows you to tackle more obstacles with less effort as time passes.

Unfortunately, what happens to many of us at the beginning of learning to deal with obstacles is we stress out and our bodies become weak. That leads to sickness, depression, obesity, and tons of other unwanted side-affects.

Important Things to Remember:

- Your purpose is the reason God sent you to earth and no one but you can do what God sent you to do. You must be brave to step into the shoes God has placed in front of you.

- When you are doing an action that is aligned with your purpose, you feel the most alive. Before you know it, you will only want to engage in actions aligned with your purpose. Being of purpose to God gives us pride that carries us through any difficult day.

- When chasing your purpose, God provides a way—always. You may think, "How can I achieve _____?" Don't worry! God will provide a way when you are working for His purpose.

Soul Work Questions:
- Do you know what your purpose is in life?

- Have your actions been aligned with your purpose? Why or why not?

- How can you help others find their purpose?

- What shift happened in your life once you found your purpose in life?

If you haven't found your purpose in life don't worry. By the time you're done reading this book you will find your purpose. For now, meditate every morning on why God sent you here.

Purpose Team Project:

Your purpose team is the group of people who guide and profoundly affect your life. These people often have similar goals and characteristics as you, yet they are also individually special. The strongest thing you have in common is your shared desire to attain your purpose and to support each other. It is key to identify your purpose people early so you can tap into their love and encouragement, and help each other along the journey of self-discovery. Purpose people are often:

- Disciplined: they practice what they preach and keep you on track.

- Ambitious: they work hard towards important goals and dreams.

- Responsible: they hold themselves and you to the best standards and give helpful advice.

Your first purpose people project is to discover and assembly your purpose people—the individuals in your life who help you grow and will keep you grounded to your goals!

Chapter 2

How Life Works

"You will begin to live your life on purpose because you will begin to love on purpose."

Before your birth, God creates "your blueprint" so you can achieve God's plan for you on earth. You and God create obstacles that will ultimately help you, and you write in people to be in your life at the right time to help you during a challenging season. The harder your "story," the bigger your purpose. If you had a horrible past, just know that God has a big purpose for you. You are intended to assist many people. Otherwise, you and God would not have placed so many obstacles in your blueprint!

Once you and God are done creating your plan, your spirit is sent to that mother's womb. When you are born, initially your spirit says, *"YES I'm here and now I can achieve my purpose and go back home to God."* You have your blueprint and you want to achieve it. However, through life's obstacles, you are forced to forget and focus on survival. You can't be who you genuinely want to be, because society forces you to dress a certain way, speak a certain way, and parents try to control who your friends are and what schools you attend, etc.

Many times we forget we have a blueprint or purpose in life because we have so much chaos to manage, i.e. domestic or sexual abuse or loss. It's difficult, if not impossible, to focus on our blueprint and purpose when we have to focus on survival. So we completely forget who we truly are and what we came here to accomplish.

We no longer validate ourselves as our parents and environment defines who we are. Nature and nurture. For example: *"Try on this outfit so I can make sure it looks cute enough for school."* Or: *"Let me see your hair to make sure it's combed right."* Eventually, kids start seeking their parents' opinion/validation/approval on everything, not just attire and hygiene. *"How does this look?"* I'm sure you've done it too. It's a terrible habit that must be broken. I stopped because I realized it wasn't an empowering question for me to ask. I stopped that negative behavior. This type of behavior does two detrimental things to children who turn into insecure, self-sabotaging adults:

1. They learn not to validate themselves and look for validation outside.
2. They grow up feeling they are not good enough to make their own decisions.

A better way to approach this dynamic to empower children is: *"Honey get dressed for school and let Mami see the nice outfit you picked out when you are done."* Or *"Beautiful; go comb your hair for school and I'll help you in a second. You always do such a great job!"*

To this day when I go shopping, and I always go alone, I put on earphones so that sales associates who are taught this horrible behavior leave me alone. That way, I can focus on my opinion. I don't need them telling me what they think does or doesn't look great on me. I want to, I need to, make my own decisions and judgments about myself.

For that same reason, I won't go to places where I know I'm not wanted. If I know someone with bad energy will be there, I'll kindly decline to spare myself the self-repair I will later need to handle the negativity they left on me.

For Example:

Me: *"So Noel, how was work?*

Them: *"Ugh I hate them all and they hate me."*

Me: *"So Noel, how is your husband?"*

Them: *"He's cheating on me and I'm going to go to that girl's house and tell her off"* and so on...

I'm sure you know who that is in your group. Or maybe it's you. I choose to not be around those types of people because I simply don't need that energy! Trust me, I've tried to convert all of the "Noels," but you can lead a horse to water but you cannot make them drink. Someone can have a million dollars but instead of being grateful for how God has blessed them, they still degrade and disrespect themselves with their words. As we get older, it doesn't get any better. Our parents evolve from telling us what to wear to pressuring us to get married and have children. They don't do it maliciously, they do it because they love us. Now we must teach them how to treat us.

This was my experience with my mom. She began pressuring me to have children, and I had to tell her that everything will happen in time. When she persisted, I had to break it down to her.

Me: *"Mami, I love you very much and I want you to understand that my purpose in life is to help many people and not just the ones I give birth to. When you give me hints about having children, the way it translates to me is that I'm not good enough for you. That doesn't empower me.*

I love you very much and I know those are not your intentions, but I have to tell you my truth because I am trying to protect my heart as much as possible now and I want you to help me. Ok?"

Her: *"Oh mijita, I'm so sorry I didn't mean it that way at all. Thank you for telling me. I won't do it again, I love you!"*

That was it! We have to re-teach people how to treat us and tell them how their words translate to us. Most people conform to the pressure and, if they're lucky, end up with a bachelor's degree that won't really do anything for them. They are in student loan and credit card debt, and just pick someone to get married and have kids with. To stop everyone from asking *"Are you married yet and do you have kids?"* On the outside, they may look happy but inside, they are empty and miserable. They feel this way because they never stopped to ask "What do I really want?" or "Who am I really?"

Good news: Some people have begun to wake up. They still don't know their purpose, but they know they are here for a reason and they want to discover that reason. I can tell people are waking up from the statistics. High divorce rates tell me people are no longer conforming to or caring less about societal standards. They have lost hope with what they have, and are in search for more.

That's why you see so many lost people out there. I call them zombies. Although their eyes and mouths are open; when you look at their eyes, you can see their spirit muted because their heart is shattered. It breaks my heart and I do everything in my power to restore that person's heart back to 100 percent health.

What Is a Zombie?

Zombies can tell you about every reality show but ask them about Ego or universal consciousness and they go back to the zombie look.

Zombies sabotage their life like "Noel." Deep inside, a zombie knows they're a zombie but they feel it's easier to remain in this state than to wake up! You must have courage and endurance to want to wake up!

To know if you are still in a zombie state, ask yourself: *"Do I need something MORE"*? This manifests in your body through: addictions, being overweight, underweight, acne, pain, insomnia, depression, hair loss, etc. If the answer is "yes," then your answer is YES!

You can be a millionaire and not know your purpose in

life, and therefore still feel empty, lonely, and miserable. Hence the saying, "Money can't buy happiness".

Once you create your blueprint board and find your purpose, you will remember the reason you came to this earth. You will once again connect with God. You will know you don't have to go to church to talk to God. God is part of you. You can speak with God whenever you want because God lives in your heart.

Forgiving Yourself

When you discover your purpose in life, you'll experience a euphoric feeling of happiness and joy. Mostly because you will see that you have already taken so many of the right steps without knowing, and that's when you begin to forgive yourself for being so mean to yourself when you were simply lost. As Maya Angelou said, if you would have known better, you would have done better.

When we forgive ourselves for judging ourselves so harshly, we begin the healing process from the inside out. That's why we feel so good. We are finally getting some medicine for those old wounds.

When we rid ourselves of the toxic feelings that manifest

into our "ugliness," our body and mind become renewed.

It takes time, but after all the toxic thoughts are flushed out of you, you will see your body transform to the best version of you. It's amazing!

The Toxic thoughts can look like this:
- I'm fat.

- I'm stupid.

- I should have gone to school.

- My friends have better lives.

- I'm not good enough.

This is what is being flushed out of your system. These are the toxic thoughts that have morphed into external toxicity, such as a double chin and hair loss and every other "ugly" thing. Remember your birth is proof that you are good enough. You are wanted and needed.

You have a purpose on this earth, and you are a blessing. You just need to wake up and realize that there is power in your words. You need to stop cursing your own life and the lives of others.

Compassion vs. Judgment

When you find your purpose, you begin to smile at strangers and say *"Good Morning"* instead of burying your head in your phone to check emails before going to the office. You will begin to play with pets and bond with them in a new way.

When you find your purpose, you will begin to look at the homeless person differently, the guy with all the tattoos on his neck differently, the woman whose dress is two sizes too small differently.

Instead of *"What is she wearing…she is too old for that,"* you will think *"Poor woman, her self-esteem must be at its lowest, I wonder what she's going through or what went on in her personal life. Let me pray for her."* Your life changes and you beg into glow from the inside and everybody notices. You no longer want to feed your body bad "food" because you know that this body is the shell for your spirit, soul, ego, and mind. They all begin to work together instead of against each other for survival. Before your Ego, Mind, and Heart would be at war inside. Once they discover that all of the fighting is causing your shell to sadden and therefore decay, they will stop fighting and work together.

So now your body will only feed itself good "food." Positive thoughts instead of bad thoughts, veggies instead of potato chips, a nice husband/wife instead of a resentful one, honest worker instead of a slacker. We begin to make better choices for our survival. The less stress and drama a.k.a. trauma for our body (ego, spirit, soul, heart, mind), the better!

You'll start to treat your body with kindness and eat healthy food, and you stop telling yourself bad things like, *"Look at that roll on your neck, you're such a pig."* Instead, you say, *"Looks like I've been having a little too much fun with snacks, let me cut back this week."* You will treat yourself with the love God intended.

When you begin to have negative thoughts of your job or your ex or someone passing away, you now say *"Is it healthy for me to choose to focus on that thought? No, so let's press delete, and let's see what's the next thought….okay, this is a good one, let's focus on this thought for a while."*

Self-Respect

Now that you know you have the Divine in you, you will begin to respect yourself in a new way. If someone disrespects you, they are also disrespecting your Divine. You will think, *"How can that person disrespect me and try to knock me off of my path to achieve my purpose? How dare they, I am doing God's work—they've got to go!"* Before, you might have given them a second or third or hundredth chance, and therefore they would have slowed you down or stopped you from achieving your purpose.

Remember, you can lead a horse to water, but you can't make it drink. If they don't want to drink, they must stop polluting your water source.

You Will Get Better Looking With Less Effort

As you treat yourself better, you will become better looking on the outside and your confidence will rise as you transform into the best version of yourself. When you experience true love for yourself, you produce feel-good endorphins because you naturally feel great and your body repairs itself.

When you're happy you take care of yourself. I'm not stressing because now I respect myself enough to rest. I go to the spa to be quiet and repair my "shell" and read my books. I take long baths now where I meditate and leave salsa music in the background. I know it's time to get out of the tub if a good song comes on. I dance in the mirror *(how God brought me to this world)* and pretend I'm at a club. I laugh at myself for being so silly. It's fun and I look forward to it! I now perform in the mirror like I'm the headliner.

Love after finding your purpose

Once you radiate happiness and health from finding your purpose, you will not know what to do with all the men (and women) who are asking you out! It's almost like people smell joy and self-love. They want a confident woman who knows what she wants and knows what she's worth. That will be you after this book.

You will begin to live your life on purpose because you will begin to love on purpose. If your family is broken for whatever reason and you haven't spoken to them, you will now be inclined to reach out because you will understand and have compassion for them.

Finding your purpose is a powerful thing!

Once you create your blueprint and find your purpose you will be able to make your dream a reality! Your blueprint board is like a review guide your teacher gave you to research and be tested. If you study, you increase your odds of achieving your purpose before you return "Home"!

For example: If I know that my calling is to act and I'm going to be offered a huge role, then I should take an acting class or two to freshen up. If I know that my calling is to be a pastor, I should read the Bible.

Once you remember your purpose you will begin to pay attention to visions or messages that God has for you, but you must find time for stillness to receive his/her visions and messages for you. For instance, let's say you get a random email about an open call audition for Dorothy in a Wizard of Oz production. You will now pay attention and consider auditioning. You will begin to pay attention to the small voice inside you, so you can stay on track and finish your tasks quicker. You will have more time to enjoy this beautiful world that was created for you!

Once you create your board and find your purpose, you will be able to spot other people, based on their energy, who have found their purpose. It's such an amazing feeling of love and unity.

Soul Work Questions:
1) Whose hindering language do you need to address and correct?

2) Are you the 99%?

3) If so, do you want to change?

4) List the degrading comments you tell yourself and debunk them.

Purpose Team Project:

Practice positive language with your purpose people! Say positive comments about each other and repeat mantras to encourage strength, such as "I am wonderful, I am confident, I am intelligent," "I can do anything I put my mind to," and "I believe I can succeed."

Chapter 3

We Learn From Hardships

"We learn the most during our hardest times"

Everything happens when it's supposed to happen. Nothing happens by coincidence or luck. Even terrible things that we call obstacles, like car accidents, miscarriages and divorces, are part of our journey for a reason.

Sometimes God reveals the reason to us immediately and sometimes we don't get the reason for years. Nonetheless, we need to trust God's plan for us and go with the flow. When we overcome obstacles, we need to shift our focus from the suffering to the lesson. It's easy for me to say this now, because I've worked hard at not suffering and simply trusting everything that happens is God's plan for me. The fastest way I've found to snap out of it is asking, *"What is something valuable than can come out of this bad situation? God, what are you directing me to?"* Many times we face horrific challenges in life like sickness, physical or sexual abuse, and abandonment. Instead of focusing on how life has cheated us, we must focus on how we can use what we learned during that dark period. How we can help others heal faster than we healed, or get out of a bad situation if we detect it. Some people may start organizations to help others cope with the same issues they dealt with growing up. Many reach back and help other girls or boys who have been abused. Many become school psychologists so they can help the students.

At their core, obstacles make us feel like it's us against the world. We start asking God bigger questions because we realize life isn't like the movies or television. We begin to demand answers.

The benefit of facing big obstacles early is we're able to go through tough times and build our emotional and spiritual strength. Soon, no obstacle can hold us down for too long and we see them as benefits.

The biggest obstacle I went through in my teens was having my parents incarcerated when I was 14 through my mid-20s. Not sure of the exact dates, as I've chosen to delete those years from my consciousness because there was too much suffering. I had no clue how life worked. I would have dinners or conversations with people and not remember any of it because the entire time, I was worrying about my parents and hoping they were fine. That obstacle helped me awaken spiritually. From that moment, I began making better choices in life. Every now and then, I would go back to "sleep" because of my depression. For a few years in high school, I felt I was in a fog just trying to keep up a strong front because no one knew the truth of my family. If they saw me down, they would ask questions. I held everything in and when I went home I would cry from the bottom of my soul. I couldn't understand why everyone else had parents and normal birthdays and holidays that I didn't experience. I was able to see my parents infrequently, and only for a few hours.

That experience made me who I am. Although I was in a fog, I was determined to win, and I maintained a 4.2 GPA. I was Best All-Around Player in volleyball and I had a full time job at a pizza restaurant to pay for my necessities. I hustled! I was motivated to leave the life I was living. I wanted a better life and I knew education was my way out. I studied until I couldn't anymore, and I surrounded myself with people who inspired me. At 18, I landed a job with millionaire Steve Harvey.

Looking back, I ask myself if I could delete the obstacle of my parents in jail, would I? No. That obstacle taught me I can achieve whatever I set my mind to, and get closer to God. What I've learned is my obstacles have made me successful.

We learn the most during our hardest times because it's during those broken moments that we reassess what life is truly about, and we reunite with God. When times are great, many people forget about what really matters and some may even forget to pray altogether. It's in those moments of darkness when you feel you have nothing left, when the only one you can turn to is God, that's when you open that channel of communication again and the lessons God teaches you are priceless.

Two years ago, a man as close to me as an uncle passed away. Nicolas worked at my parents' store from the time I was six years old. I adored him. When I grew older, I would drive Nicolas home after his shifts and we would bond over salsa music. He taught me the history and background of each song and told me about his earlier life in Cuba. He came to America to help others, as he felt that was his life's purpose. He wore white every single day of his life. He was kind to everyone he met and he always wore a big smile on his face.

Once I started going to USC, I lost touch with him. Eventually when I came back to Los Angeles after living in New York, I started visiting him again. I would go to his house and just talk with him for a while. I loved knocking on his door and yelling "Nicolassss." He would always recognize my voice and say "Elviraaaaahija hay voy" and he would open the door with such joy.

When he passed, I learned many lessons. One was to never be sad when someone passes away, because they went to be with God. Another was to know they never intended to be here always, but to just be here long enough to do God's work and return Home. I remember at his funeral I felt joy because it was so beautiful. If you haven't gone to a Cuban funeral, you must attend one because it is the most beautiful and spiritual send-off with drums, singing, dancing, and good food. I could feel his Spirit in the room!

I also learned, through his life, to live for God and nothing else. When I was upset over breakups, he always told me to focus on what God wanted for me versus what I was being stubborn about. Nicolas was such an amazing soul on this earth. I feel privileged to have spent time with him.

Being Broken Simply Means You Are Going To Be Renewed.

When we are renewed we are fully able to recall who we truly are and what we are intended to do on earth. It's not until we are broken that we accept a new way of thinking. The fact that you are breaking is a blessing that gives you a head start. Yes, it hurts to be broken, but it only lasts a little while. The knowledge and wisdom you get from it is worth the pain!

Just like my journey. I could have chosen to stick to my 9-5 schedule and live like a zombie and wake up in my old age to say, *"What did I do with my life?"* Instead, I chose hard obstacles to get my awakening much sooner, so I can help the rest of you awaken!

Soul Work Questions:

- Do you have the courage to wake up NOW?

- Do you take time to be in silence so you can hear God?

- When did God break you? How did God break you? Was it through illness, parents' divorce, personal illness, parents' death? What woke you up?

- When you were broken, did you rebuild your relationship with God? How so?

Soul Work Guidance:

- Ask God to reveal the lessons to you.

- Shift your focus to your purpose versus your obstacle.

- Find positive go-to's, like hiking, praying, meditating, yoga, working out, comedy, etc., when you are feeling down so you are able to shift your focus.

- Let go of any guilt you may have for things in the past. Everything we go through in life is intended for our good.

- When obstacles happen don't get upset; focus on finding the lesson and a solution. All obstacles are put in our path to either redirect us or to teach us a lesson we need in order to succeed.

- Are you able to easily hear God? If yes, fantastic! If you're not able to yet, don't worry, I have an entire chapter dedicated to this topic. In the meantime, work on clearing out all of your internal chaos. Once you do this, you will be able to hear God much clearer and louder. This will help in suffering less when obstacles occur. God immediately gives you the intended lessons and redirection.

Purpose Team Project:

With your purpose team, talk about a time you went through an obstacle and how you overcame it, as well as any lessons you learned from it. Brainstorm ways to overcome and learn from common obstacles such as losing a loved one, financial hardship, and physical injuries.

Chapter 4

We Have Power

"We are supposed to go through life knowing our blueprint and enjoying life because this world is for enjoyment and love"

We co-create our life with God before we are conceived in our mother's womb. We do this because we have the Divine in us and always have access to a higher consciousness that holds all the answers we need. God sends us messages or signs and we are to follow that guidance. In doing this we are co-creating our life with our creator.

Opportunities don't just arise, we create them with God! Every opportunity in my life is one *we* created. My Steve Harvey opportunity is a great example. God sent me a sign to tune in to a certain radio station. I obeyed. When I was listening to the radio show on my way to college, Steve Harvey said if anyone wanted to attend their in-studio audience taping, fax-in a request. At that moment, I got a feeling in my stomach and that translated to faxing in my request. God let me know at that moment that there was something at that radio station for me. I didn't have plans to ask for a job that day; it just happened. As they were letting the audience leave, I got another hunch to go and ask for a job. Instead of denying my intuition, I followed it. That day I landed an internship that eventually led to a full-time job with Steve Harvey. Had God not sent me those feelings and signs I would have never even tuned in to that radio station nor would I have faxed in my request to attend the taping.

Many of us receive signs all the time but we are so busy in our lives we neglect to see them. We have to make sure we're always paying attention and in communication with God so we can receive guidance. We are supposed to go through life knowing our blueprint and enjoying life because this world is for enjoyment and love. Instead, since we've forgotten all about our blueprint, we go through life killing ourselves with stress that leads to cancer, heart attacks, and more noise. God would never have sent us to this side without letting us know our purpose. Over time we forgot it and now it is our mission to find it and pursue it.

Knowing your purpose in life feels amazing! You begin to have a tremendous trust in God because you know everything that happens in your life is for your greater good. You just have to unscramble the puzzle.

There are many ways to find your purpose in life, but one prerequisite is you must have a healthy and open heart so that you can listen to God and be guided. Many people walk around depressed, disillusioned, abandoned, hurt, and abused. They are stuck in their pain and don't realize they have a purpose because their pain is blocking their ability to hear God. The best thing to do if you can't hear God is start thinking positive.

For example, whenever I'm starting to feel negative or sad, I ask myself, *"What are some things I'm proud of?"* I start saying things that make me feel good about what I've done in this world. I automatically feel much better! When I'm feeling terrible, I immediately go to the mountains and run, and in minutes I'm able to shift my energy back to positive so I am able to hear God fully.

Symptoms of People Who Do Not Know Their Purpose

People who are angry, evil, abusive, resentful, depressed, a.k.a. "Debby Downers," are negative because they do not know their purpose. When your heart is healthy, it's impossible to express negativity in any form.

It doesn't have to be a person who hurts your heart. It can be an event, a death, a rape, a fraud, an ex…our past! For example, I couldn't do anything huge with my life because my heart was broken the night my sister called and told me my parents were sentenced to 20 years to life for selling drugs. I said *"What are you talking about, they don't sell drugs?!"* I remember throwing that phone against the wall and seeing all of those pieces scatter on the floor. That's exactly how I felt my heart was: broken and scattered all over the floor. I didn't know where to begin to put the pieces back together.

That event shattered me for a while. At 14 years old, I was left feeling abandoned, alone, inadequate, and unprotected. It manifested into: bad relationships, illness, low self-esteem, and depression. Even if we tape our heart back together it's not until we control the issues that we can super glue it back. I was incredibly depressed during those days. I didn't understand why God would give me such a tough obstacle. What I now realize is God didn't do it *to* me but *for* me! That obstacle has been the biggest blessing in my life. I got closer to God and I learned I'm capable of much more than I ever imagined. Obstacles sometimes lead us to meeting people we have sacred agreements with. A sacred agreement is someone God has put in our life to learn lessons from or get guidance through. You'll know when you meet a sacred agreement when: you get goose bumps and it's like your hearts are smiling at each other. When you feel you knew them in another life or you are supposed to do something great with them in this life.

Sometimes people you have sacred agreements with can annoy or hurt you. For example, if you are working with someone and you can't stand them, they still teach you a lot and you just know they are intended to be in your life. That's a sacred agreement when it looks ugly. Those people are not intended to stay in our life forever, just long enough to learn our lesson from them.

How to find the Lesson

When you communicate with your sacred agreement, pay attention to what they say. If they invite you to an event, go. The odds are that something great may happen. If you need guidance in something they are experts, try and meet them in person to see if there are additional signs and guidance they can give you.

How to know when a Sacred Agreement season is over

You will know your time together is over because of the energy the other person gives you. For example, if you have been emailing this person and every time they respond within 24 hours and for the last 2-3 months they don't respond to your emails or texts or calls know that the season is done. This is not meant to hurt you but to let you know that there is nothing left to learn from them. You must now go out and find another mentor to learn from.

If you are in a sacred agreement and that person converts to Bad Energy let them go as a friend/mentor! Negative energy is contagious and you do not want to have anyone or anything mess with your energy you've worked so hard to protect.

Think about people who have come into your life and instantly impacted you and gave you chills you when met them. The people who have given you advice and helped redirect your path. These are the people with whom you have sacred agreements. You know them from another lifetime or you are supposed to do something with them in this lifetime. Their energy seems very familiar to you and you feel comfortable around them instantly.

These feelings are genuine! Also, when the opposite happens, know that the universe is giving you clear signs that you are not supposed to work with those people. Always follow your intuition.

Below is an exercise I'd like you to try so you can get clarity on who you have sacred agreements with. This will help you in creating your blueprint board.

Soul Work Suggestion:

- Write down names of people in your life with whom you feel you have a sacred agreement.
- Write down what qualities they have that you aspire to have.
- What did they teach you?
- How did they redirect you in your journey?
- List ways you notice you've co-created your life.
    a. Examples: How did you meet your husband?
    b. How did you get into college?
    c. How did you meet your best friend?
    d. How did you land your job?
- Are you comfortable being alone? Why or why not? Have you thanked the people you have sacred agreements with for being part of your journey?
- If not, do so this week via email, letter, phone call or lunch. It's great to stay in touch with this core group. Simply let them know that you appreciate what they did for you and that you are aware they didn't have to do it. Let them know that because they did that for you, you will now help someone else and it's all because of them!

Purpose Team Project:

Tell each of your purpose people why they are important in your life and what they have taught you. Share their best qualities with

others and find someone to help just as they have helped you.

Chapter 5

Energy

"Only surround yourself with other good-energy people"

When it comes to energy, Albert Einstein put it best. "Everything is energy and that's all there is to it. Match the frequency of the reality you want and you cannot help but get that reality. It can be no other way. This is not philosophy. This is physics."

Every person is made up of energy and we all radiate a vibration according to our frequency. For example, a person who spends their days praying, fasting, meditating will be vibrating at a higher energy frequency than a person who spends their days at work fighting with customers. Clearly, the first person will be attracting good things into their life whereas the second person will attract more fights and chaos in their life. In order to attract great things into our life we need to vibrate at a higher frequency so our prayers manifest quicker. Below are a few keys on how you can get your energy to a frequency where you are now attracting versus repelling opportunities and good fortune:

1) Surround yourself with positive people.

2) When obstacles arise never ask "why me" but rather look for the lesson.

3) Always try and keep the peace with family, friends, clients, co-workers. Negativity aimed towards you can block your roads.

4) Meditate.

5) Pray.

6) Have no-talk days where you deal with internal chaos for the week so that you don't carry weeks, months, and years of baggage on your soul.

7) Be in nature.

One of the most important keys is to surround yourself with high frequency people. Definitely date and marry someone with good energy. Ninety percent of your success depends on whom you marry. We need to be around people who inspire, uplift, and motivate us to be our best self. People with bad energy suck all of the light out of the good energy people. Before we know it we're thinking negative and vibrating at a low frequency just like them. We must get these people out of our lives if we truly want to succeed.

Only surround yourself with other good-energy people. You will know who they are by how you feel around them. People with good energy only want to uplift you and enjoy your company. High frequency people are not there to bring you down in any way, shape, or form.

People with bad energy have had obstacles in life too. Instead of learning to use them as stepping stones, they hurt others because of the pain they've felt. The saying by Will Bowen is true: *"Hurt people hurt people. We are not being judgmental by separating ourselves from such people. But we should do so with compassion. Compassion is defined as a "keen awareness of the suffering of another coupled with a desire to see it relieved." People hurt others as a result of their own inner strife and pain. Avoid the reactive response of believing they are bad; they already think so and are acting that way. They aren't bad; they are damaged and they deserve compassion. Note that compassion is an internal process, an understanding of the painful and troubled road trod by another. It is not trying to change or fix that person."*

If we don't want to get hurt in any way, we must separate ourselves from people who only aim to hurt us.

Soul Work Suggestions:

- Is there anyone in your life you have to let go because their energy is toxic to you?

- Are you a negative person? If yes, what are some changes you can make to change that?

- Does your family criticize others?

- Do you criticize yourself often? If yes, write down 10 great qualities about you.

Purpose Team Project:

Meditate together and focus on gaining good energy. Go around in the group to say positive things about your day, and what has been a particularly positive thing you have recently experienced. Bask in the glow of warm memories and happy thoughts.

Chapter 6

Take Control Of Your Thoughts

"We manifest what we think about the most"

Our mind is incredibly powerful. What we think we manifest. Many people think it's what we say or write that matters most, but in fact what matters most are the thoughts that run through our mind. Every minute, we have 35-48 thoughts and whichever of those thoughts are recurring or dominant is what you will create in the future.

Let's say a wealthy woman begins to think pessimistically and she loses her confidence. She can be sure to lose her wealth. It was because of her certainty and positivity that she was blessed with wealth in the first place. If she loses her principles, she will lose what she manifested.

We've also heard opposite stories where the poor guy

dreams of riches and starts to visualize his success. The next thing he knows, he has manifested it. It's the law of the universe: we manifest what we think about the most. So if we want a positive life, we need to think positive. If we want to be wealthy, we need to think wealthy thoughts. If we want to have the best body in the world, we better stop body-shaming ourselves.

What we focus on will grow. If we choose to focus on negative thoughts that will produce a negative life. Have you ever had a friend tell you they've had the most terrible day and things keep getting worse? They have all of that negative energy in them—it's no wonder things keep turning out bad. At the moment of the first obstacle, they needed to release the negative energy and just think, *"If this is done, it has to be for my good, so I will continue with a positive and great day!"*

We are human and we will continue to have those pesky negative thoughts that keep popping up, because our brain is so used to negative thoughts it's almost addicted to them. What we have trained our brain to do, it will do. Now that you know you can control your brain say this, *"Nope I don't like that thought of my ex-boyfriend cheating on me delete that's over, next*

thought...." And keep doing that every time and before you know

it those thoughts will be gone because you no longer accept them.

It's a choice we have always had. It's possible to control your

thoughts. No thought is more powerful than us! We have the

power to select what we focus on. So focus on the positive. Focus

on things that are important and which will cause you joy and

success. Channel your energy into working towards your goals,

and refuse to let others bring you down. Especially with their

words, keep repeating the old mantra, "sticks and stones will break

my bones, but words will never hurt me."

Don't let words hurt you, and definitely don't use them to

hurt other people. Choose your words wisely and use them to

communicate well. From positive thoughts to positive words, your

actions and self-image will become more positive.

Soul Work Assignment

- What are negative thoughts you have of yourself that you
  want to get over?

- What mistakes have you made that haunt you? Can you forgive yourself today and promise to do better?

- What is a positive thought you can always refer to?

- What is a mantra you can say when you are feeling negative or depressed to snap you out of it? Mine is "With God all things are possible" when I feel something is impossible and "God loves me" when I feel insecure and "I shall fear nothing but God" when I'm scared.

Purpose Team Project:

Share and practice your positive mantras with your purpose people. Do an arts and crafts activity where you write or paint out your mantra as a poster/sign/painting/framed quote/etc. Display your artful mantras somewhere you can see and repeat them every day.

Chapter 7

Clear Out the Chaos

"It takes a lot of courage to sit down with the thoughts that haunt us, but it's well worth it"

No one would be talking, yet I would hear so much dialogue. Slowly I had to make peace with all the voices I heard yelling at me. I would hear constantly *"Are you happy", "Are you doing the right thing in life", "You're not successful enough", "Why don't you have a boyfriend, you must be a bad person", "Are you ever going to have children,"* and more annoying things I felt I couldn't manage. I tried going to a therapist to talk it out and although it was nice, what I really needed to do was answer all of those voices so they can shut up. I would initially get upset with them and then I'd feel bad. When they came back, I did the same thing, never dealing with what that meant to me. Once I finally sat with every thought, my inner chaos was gone! I could finally sleep at night without tossing and turning. I was finally able to go to a spa and sit there for hours because now those thoughts weren't haunting me. Typically, when those thoughts would come, I would turn up the radio and sing loud so I couldn't hear them or I would start reading a book because the mind can't think and read at the same time. I found tons of solutions but sitting still with those thoughts was not an option for me for many years. It's no wonder I couldn't hear God.

Those thoughts were so loud God couldn't get through to me. Now that I've cleared out all of my internal chaos I can hear God loud and clear. When I feel internal chaos, I deal with it immediately because I don't want it to affect my relationship with God and I don't want to operate from a hurt/mad place. I always want to operate from a loving and kind place.

The only way I can do that is if I don't have internal chaos. It takes a lot of courage to sit down with the thoughts that haunt us, but it's well worth it. Now I enjoy going to the spa alone so that I can sit and talk to God. I feel like hours are minutes and I feel tremendous joy, where before I felt enormous emotional pain.

There are a lot of people who are addicted to chaos. They can go to a nice dinner and because they are addicted to chaotic energy, they will find a way to create it. They will either find a problem with the menu, waiter, restaurant, or something. Innately, they feel happiness when they have chaos. That is a sad dynamic because they are simply attracting negativity and bad fortune into their lives.

Soul Work Suggestions:

1) What internal chaos do you have that you need to get rid of? Sit for an hour with no phone, TV, or radio and write down all the negative thoughts that come to your mind. Once the hour is over review the list and debunk each with a positive thought or affirmation. This will begin to re-direct your brain to positive thoughts versus negative.

2) Are you okay being still/alone for long periods of time? If not, try simply walking at the park/mountains for 15 minutes without anyone or your phone.

3) The next time you are feeling internal chaos what are some steps you can take to deal with it so it doesn't affect your

life?

Purpose People Project:

Relax with your purpose people! Do a fun activity, such as a trip, a game night, a party, a cooking class, a movie-watching night, etc., anything and everything that releases pent-up negative energy and gets out the positive vibes. In addition to your fun group activity for relaxation, practice group meditation to maximize your positive energy.

Chapter 8

Create Your Blueprint Board

"Who you have attracted to your life will let you know who you are supposed to be."

I'm going to show you how to find out who you supposed to be, based on whom God put in your life. I will then give you the template to create your own.

Who Your Mentors and Guides Are:
Mentor- is someone who gives you guidance on your journey
Guide- someone who redirects your path

Step #1 you will need the following:

1) White presentation board with 3 main sections. You can purchase them at any Staples or Office Depot.

2) Scissors

3) Glue or Tape

4) Pen

5) Highlighters

6) Black Sharpie

7) Printer

8) Computer

Step #2 Print Images

You will need to print full-body images of your family. Print

an image of yourself when you are smiling big! I would

suggest choosing the nicest images of your mentors/guides and

family so if they see it one day they are flattered.

Take pride in your board!

Step #3 Title the sections

Section 1-Family

Section 2- Mentors and Guides I Chose Unconsciously

(section2 should be the section with the biggest amount of

space)

Section 3- Patterns I notice

Section 1-Family

Paste the images of your family:

Dad-

Mom-

Sibling 1-

Sibling 2-

& etc.

I had you print full body images of them since you will need more space on the board to write their information. So make sure you spread them out.

Next to their pictures write and then fill in the information:
   a) Name

   b) Birthday

   c) Best quality

   d) Weak quality

   e) Lesson they taught you in life

   f) Anti-Lesson you learned from their life

   g) What is their life result because of their life choices?

Section 2- Mentors and Guides

Paste the images of yourself at the top of the board and on top of that put your name and your birthday. Then paste the images of the faces of your guides and mentors in the order that you met them and number them.

Next to their pictures write and then fill in the information:
  a) Name

  b) Birthday

  c) What did they teach you or how did they redirect you?

Section 3-Patterns
In this section write:
  1) Family's Occupations- List the professions, not the names.

  2) Mentors' and Guides' Occupations- List the professions, not the names.

  3) Based on them, who are you?

Did you have your AHA moment?! Did you realize who you are intended to be based on your team? Who you are and have been become 100 percent clear, and it begins to get clearer and clearer from this point on! Who you have attracted to your life will let you know who you are supposed to be. Whatever number of guides/mentors you have now is great. You can always add guides/mentors in the future. Now that you know how it works you will carefully select who you want to be your next guide or mentor. You do not have to use all of your mentors/guides for your team. Be selective with who you want to work and build with. Some mentors are in your life for many chapters and others are just there for a few. Also, some mentors may relocate or move, so make sure the team you assemble is something that is realistic based on location.

Step # 3 Reflect On Your Relationships

When I meditated on my blueprint board, I realized there was a reason my parents were incarcerated. Had this not happened, I would have never gone to Mt. Sac, I would have never met Erica on the volleyball team, who linked me to a job that had a fax machine. Had I not had that job, I would have never been able to request tickets to The Steve Harvey Morning Show. Everything happens for a reason. Reflect on your board. How did you get HERE?

Prepare For The Breakthrough

Knowing that you will soon have a big breakthrough, you must prepare for it!

Soul Work Questions:

1) Meditate while looking at the board for several minutes each day until it becomes 100% clear to you.

You have to rid yourself of the people that may block (distract/steer you away/hinder/sabotage) you from your Purpose.

Example:

Her: *"Hi Elvira, the girls and I are going out for drinks and we want to invite you!"*

Me: *"Thank you so much for thinking of me, but I'm finishing my book. Enjoy! I'll be out soon."*

Her: *"No problem, get 'em girl! I will pray for you so that many people can be blessed with your book. Holler if you want a drive-by martini."*

KEEPER!

Example of the same situation with a bad energy person: *"Why are you always such a drag...you are 29 not 92!"*

NOT A KEEPER.

Once you clear all the negative people and things out of your life you will be surprised how much better you will feel! When you encounter a negative person you will be able to spot them quickly and avoid them. Life is too short to hang out with people who will bring your energy down.

Purpose Team Project:

Share your blueprint boards with each other, and have your purpose people help you figure out what the ultimate blueprint of your life points toward. Comment on each other's boards (make them together as a bonding and relaxing activity!) and find ways to strengthen positive ties and cut toxic ones.

Chapter 9

Having A Healthy Heart Is Important

"Although at times in our life we feel we can't hear God, we must know that God is always with us"

Our heart is where God lives in us and where our soul resides. It is the speaker that must be 100 percent in order for you to hear God clearly. Having a healthy heart is key for a purpose driven life. God can only speak to us when our heart is healthy. Think of your heart as a speaker. If the speaker is broken, shattered or unplugged, then you will not be able to hear God and receive the visions and messages you need to move forward.

You'll notice people with a healthy heart because you can feel their energy a mile away. They believe in divine order, don't judge others or themselves, and are kind to everyone they encounter. You'll notice people with broken hearts because they will not be dressed well, and will be negative about everything and everyone because at their core they are damaged.

When your speaker is hindered you must repair it ASAP so you may once again gain communication to God.

Heart Damage

25% - You are still devastated over a divorce, molestation, childhood abuse or abandonment, relative passing, business loss, etc. Because your heart is shattered and you can only hear 25%, God is barely able to reach you via signs. It's harder for you to get big opportunities because you're not tuned in.

50% - You begin to wake up because God is able to get through a little more and you ask yourself the big questions. This is when your awakening happens.

75%- You begin to manifest things with your thoughts and you begin to understand the power of your mind. You begin to select positive thoughts and work through your internal chaos.

100%- You have overcome many obstacles but you can hear God clearly. You are able to turn every misfortune into something positive. God begins to reward you for being obedient. This is when you have to work to keep your heart 100 percent healthy. My heart didn't become 100 percent healthy until I turned 29. It took me a while to get my heart's health from 30 percent to 100 percent. I did that by loving myself, and every little compliment helped!Here is an example of what I would say to myself to get my energy up and begin healing: *"Hey girl you look goooooooood today, I see ya!"* That was another 2 percent added. We exude that extra energy on the outside. Every time I took myself to the spa to thank my body for hanging in there, I added another 4 percent to my number. When I made peace with my siblings, I added a big 20 percent.

Little by little, I got here and now I make sure my heart is healthy all the time so I can hear God. I want to hear God because I want to be of service. How can I be of service if I cannot hear my Boss? I need to be at my best always for God!

Be "YOUR" Best

At *your best* means treat yourself nicely. Eat healthy, take care of yourself and get your hair done, toes, nails, and take time to meditate each day. Tell yourself that you love yourself and be proud of who you have become!

God Never Leaves Us

Although at times in our life we feel we can't hear God, we must know that God is *always* with us. We have to work hard to be able to hear God.

Once our heart is 100 percent healthy, we are able to point out others who have healthy hearts simply by their attitude/response to others and themselves. When you become broken or shattered, pick out the LESSON, feel the pain, and move on! You must be ready to fully feel the pain NOW or it will continue to make your life and body ugly.

How To Regain a 100% Healthy Heart

It's very important you find out who shattered your heart because you will need to meet with them or call them to ask them some very important questions for closure.

Let's say your father shattered your heart because he was never there for you. Your task is to contact him and ask him to dinner and ask him these questions:

1) Tell me about yourself (with a big smile and an open heart)

2) Why did you choose not to be a part of my life? (stern, not sarcastic and look into his eyes)

3) Did you ever think about contacting me? (get your why not)

4) Tell him that you forgive him for not being there and that you will not hold any resentment towards him from this moment on. Tell him you will work on forgiving him because you want to heal.

5) Give him a big hug and leave knowing that if he knew better, he would do better. No one is perfect, including parents. We all have parents who make mistakes.

Each situation is unique, but make sure you ask yourself the key questions that your heart needs to know to achieve closure. After the meeting, your joy will increase tremendously and you will once again be *you* because you will finally have let it go!

If the person who hurt you has passed away or you cannot find them, you can still get closure. Write down the questions you want to ask, and look in the mirror and into your eyes and wait for the response in your heart. God will tell you their answer. You can also do this by going to church and praying. I personally go to the beach to meditate and speak to God. It really works!

Soul Work Questions:

1) Who shattered your heart? Write down how in detail.

2) Relive it and this time feel the pain ALL the way and write it down in detail. We tend to skip the pain and go straight to the suffering. But if you truly feel the pain there is no place for the suffering when you go through traumatizing events. You must recall the incident where your heart was.

Purpose Team Project:

Tell your purpose people about the time your heart got shattered. Experience the emotional rollercoaster again with them, whether it is through acting out the event or discussing it with them. Show each other how it is possible to pick yourself up and keep going again after tragic heartbreak.

Chapter 10

Love Yourself & Heal

"We have to surrender to the fact that we are in constant transition and being different is okay"

Loving ourselves is a task for many of us. That pesky negative voice in our head is constantly telling us we're too fat, skinny, short, ugly, dumb…those thoughts are very toxic to our system. It's not until we fully love ourselves that we can finally control those thoughts in our mind.   Many of us were not taught to love ourselves properly. Typically, we love ourselves the way our parents or guardians loved us. If they constantly told you that you were smart and beautiful you will most likely grow up believing that. If your parents told you that you are not going to amount to anything and that you are stupid, then odds are you will believe that too. It's not until we grow older that we begin to validate ourselves versus letting others determine our worth.

Like everyone else, I struggle with loving myself. Like

most of you, I have been manipulated into thinking that beauty is a size 2, blond hair, and perfect skin. So when I didn't meet those requirements, I felt terrible. Now I understand that beauty comes in all shapes and sizes and colors. When I'm 10 pounds' overweight, instead of being upset at myself and anger eating, I say *"okay chica, time to cut down on all of the sweets."* No matter what our outside looks like we have to love ourselves fully so we may heal. Some people stop loving themselves when they enter relationships where the other person is constantly pointing out their flaws. Over time the person accepts the other person's claims as fact and they feel terrible about themselves. Verbal abuse is one of the most damaging things that can happen to a person. The bounce back takes time and therapy.

    This happened to one of my clients who had a relationship with a high-profile celebrity. Not only was he verbally abusive, he was a cheater and he was physically abusive as well. Her self-esteem was so low she wanted him back after he left her. We *must* carefully select our partners. We must partner with those who help and uplift our spirit instead of crush it. My mom is a perfect example of someone who fully loves herself. Since I was young, I remember my mom taking forever get ready to leave the house. She needed to always have her makeup, hair, and nails done perfectly. This included her workout sessions. She believes in looking her best always and that's so great to see. She inspires me.

My mom has taught me to love myself and to take pride in my appearance because we represent God. It's because of her that I walk with my head high and shoulders back. I've seen her do it all my life.

Not too long ago, I met up with one of my collegiate friends. She's now a professor and I'm so proud of her. We got on the topic of self-love and she said she has struggled because she has a round face and she would get teased about it. She now accepts and loves it. I told her that I too have always felt bad because I've had a chubby face since I was young and no matter how skinny my body was, my cheeks wouldn't go away. After hearing her similar insecurity, I realized I wasn't alone. I've never been told, *"No, I can't date you because you have a fat face,"* so I think I'm okay.

Being able to relate to others heals our heart. Throughout the journey we will encounter self-esteem obstacles, and at some point we have to surrender to the fact that we are in constant transition and being different is okay. So what if you are losing your hair—become the sexiest bald guy people have ever seen and own it! Who cares if you've lost a few pounds because of your sickness—go shopping for new clothes and rock it! Nothing is forever and we should enjoy every second of our journey.

Self-Love Schedule:

Here are some ideas and a sample schedule for how you can love and appreciate yourself each and every day!

8 AM: Rise and shine! Wake up and exercise a bit to move your muscles and get the blood flowing. Reflect on the beautiful day and the marvelous luck of your existence. Meditate and put yourself in a positive space to succeed today.

9 AM.: Eat a good and healthy breakfast to provide your body with the fuel it needs to succeed. While eating, you can multitask by listening to inspirational videos or reading motivational stories.

10 AM-5 PM: Many people spend this time at work, so if you're working, try to succeed at your job! Socialize with your coworkers, help others, and find ways you can improve your office space. Bring your positive energy to work and always wear a smile—people notice!

6 PM: After work, prepare a healthy dinner to wind down. If you're with family, spend time with them, or relax with friends.

7 PM: Continue spreading the love with family and friends, or use this time to improve yourself through reading/research/relaxation.

8-10 PM: Use this time for self-reflection and self-love. Do something you love, whether it's watching your favorite show, reading a new book, cooking a meal for the next day, etc.

11 PM: Get ready for bed. Say your night prayers/meditation, and envision good things for the next day. Write down your reflections on today and your goals for tomorrow.

Soul Work Questions:

- What toxic beliefs about yourself do you want to eliminate? The next time you have those thoughts say "next thought" and think of a positive memory or thought of the future.

- What can you do to show yourself self-love? Some great ways may be to go get your hair or nails done or to sleep 8 hours or eat healthy.

- What do you need to forgive yourself? Have you made a mistake that haunts you?

Purpose Team Project:

Brainstorm self-love suggestions, and then carry them out! Have a group session where you share positive things and ways to work what you have—create good memories so you can counter bad memories.

Chapter 11

Forgive Yourself & Others

"Many people think forgiving is for the other person, but truly it's for the person doing the forgiving"

Forgiveness is one of the most powerful things in this world, but it's not exercised by many. I'm sure you know people who have not talked to each other for 20 years. When you ask them why they haven't spoken, they can't remember the original reason. It's their ego not letting them put down their guard and accepting that perhaps there was fault on both sides. Yes, work has to be done to repair the relationship, but every relationship needs work to establish and maintain.

I was hurt in a past relationship when I needed surgery to remove a huge cyst on my ovary. My boyfriend at the time left me for a much younger woman who looked very much like me. I felt he quickly replaced me and he never truly loved me. I believed our entire relationship was a lie and that broke me. On top of being in physical pain, I was also in emotional pain from the breakup. A few years later, once I fully recovered, he came knocking on my door asking for forgiveness and for my hand in marriage. As angry as I was at him, I opened the door and we spoke. I told him that I forgave him but I couldn't marry him. What he did to me was something I could never bounce back from to repair our relationship. Many people think forgiving is for the other person, but truly it's for the person doing the forgiving. I didn't want to have that hate in my heart because it would affect future relationships. I also didn't want him in my life because I would constantly be reminded of the nightmare I lived during those days.

I've also been emotionally hurt in my career. Several years ago, one of my clients refused to pay my branding fee for an idea they took from me. We decided to part ways. Initially, I was devastated because I couldn't understand their dishonest behavior. Because they didn't have the contacts they needed in order to fully succeed in the business, I knew they would eventually return. Sure enough, they returned, apologized, and paid me my percentage. We continued to do business together, and have made lots of money together! I decided to forgive them because I knew they were going through a very rough time financially and they needed the money. Once they returned, I told them to be honest about their situation in the future instead of doing something shady and they agreed.

Here are a few questions you can ask yourself to see who you need to forgive:

- Who has hurt me in my childhood, in my adolescence, in my adult life?
- How do I feel about them?
- Have I forgiven them yet?
- What would it take for me to forgive each of them? Do I need an apology or do I need to release it and pray on it?

In our lives, there will be a lot of people who hurt us. Intentionally or otherwise; we have to learn to deal with it. We can't do something stupid and end up dead or in jail. We have to rationalize why the person is doing that act.

Growing up, my uncle David would come to our house every 3-4 months and try to kill my mom and anyone else in the house. He would bring a knife. My uncle was bipolar and he didn't like to take his medication. He thought nothing was wrong with him when he was normal. But once he entered the manic phase of the illness, he was in trouble, and so were we. However, I learned to forgive my uncle. Unfortunately, he stabbed himself and died when I was 16, but I still consider him to be one of my favorite uncles and I know he loved me. Forgiveness means you don't have to agree with the person's actions, but you have compassion for them and are able to let go.

Soul Work Questions:

- Who do you need to forgive and why?

- What are some steps you can take to forgive those who have hurt you?

- What are your thoughts on therapy to get beyond emotional or physical traumas?

Purpose Team Project:

Tell your purpose team about someone you need to forgive. Ask their advice on how to forgive them and move forward. After you have forgiven the person, tell your purpose people about the experience and reflect upon it as a group.

Chapter 12

When You Help Others, God Will Help You

"Failure is not fatal, it's simply the best lesson we will ever get."

The best way to help yourself is to help another person who needs exactly what you are lacking. There is always someone who is in a worse position than you that you can help. Do it! Somehow God and the universe become aware and almost immediately help you in return.

I'm very fortunate that my day job is at a publicity company where I have the ability to help others all day long. I feel it's because of my constant work to help others that God has abundantly blessed me! Had I worked in a job where I'm constantly taking from people or punishing people versus helping people, I know my karma would be much different. I walk around expecting good things to happen to me because I truly believe I'm a good person. I believe the Bible where it states that all things will be done for those who are doing God's purpose. I have tremendous confidence that everything I do will succeed because I keep God first in all projects. For example, if my clients make tons of money from a book or a movie, you can bet I'm the first one saying, *"Congratulations! Now can we start an organization to _____"* and I give them a stern look or sound over the phone and they know that if they don't, I won't open any more doors for them. When many enter the industry they don't understand this universal law. I have to teach them that if you do not give back from the blessing God has given you, God will no longer bless you. The entire reason we are being blessed is to bless others. We cannot miss the lesson in the blessing.

Many people believe they have to be perfect to help another person. That's not true. I have tons of flaws and I don't let them stop me from doing my best to help others. It's because of my flaws I can be of service to others. I've fallen many times and I've learned to get up quickly. I see many people who stay down when they fall, because they're embarrassed or don't feel they can try again and succeed. God put me on this earth to tell everyone we can all get back up and succeed! Failure is not fatal; it's simply the best lesson we will ever get.

Soul Work Questions:

- Are you helping at least one person a day? If not, how can you change that?

- Many give the church a percentage of their salary and others start foundations and directly help organizations/people who need assistance. How are you blessing others with what God has blessed you?

- Helping others can be taking an hour out and giving someone advice.

- Mentoring others and allowing them to shadow you is a great way of helping others.

- Simply saying a prayer for someone you see walking down the street who is having trouble waking is a wonderful way to help others.

- Giving someone a compliment when you see them looking down is a fantastic way of being of service.

Purpose Team Project:

Choose a charitable activity, such as volunteering at an animal shelter/soup kitchen/juvenile hall/etc., and do it as a group! Not only is this a bonding and relaxing activity, it is also a way to give back and help others. Complete and reflect on your charitable experience. If you're feeling ambitious, try to make it a regular activity!

Chapter 13

Transitioning from Career To Purpose

"God blesses those of us who are courageous enough to stray from the norm and focus on fulfilling His plan"

None of us were born with a career, but we were all born with a purpose! A career is something our parents and our society force upon us. Our Purpose is what God intends us to be when we were sent here. For many of you who are still in your pursuit, I will explain further to provide ultimate clarity.

Career versus Purpose

Many of us had or have dreams of becoming doctors or lawyers because we were persuaded that those were the careers that confirmed you made it and your parents did their job. But let's be honest, how many terrible doctors and lawyers have you met? I bet those were the people that wanted to please their parents or prove something to society, but their purpose is far from their career.

A career will provide you money, but your purpose will give you happiness and ultimately financial freedom, because GOD blesses those who are courageous enough to stray from the norm and focus on fulfilling His plan.

Making The Transition

To transition from a career-driven life to a purpose-driven life, you must first create a plan! Let's say you work from 9-5, Monday-Friday. From now on, you will have another job from 6-10 pm on weekdays and 9-5 pm on the weekend that's called your Purpose. Initially, it will be challenging because you will have to give up a lot to make this transition happen. Whatever you do for your purpose must generate income so you can start your purpose. This can be extra paid hours at your current job or side jobs to generate revenue.

The goal is to save 6 months of your overhead so that you have the freedom in the near future to work on your purpose all day/everyday without having to worry about finances for at least 6 months. You will also need to save your start-up expenses. For example, if you are going to switch from an attorney to an author, you will need to calculate how much it will cost to release your first book. If you are going to be a person who builds and create transitional housing for abused women, you will need to calculate how much it will cost to build your first facility.

While you're saving make sure to read and research as much as possible. Also build your purpose muscles so once it's time, you are ready to go. For instance, if you're going to be a motivational speaker, practice and build your relationships so once you are financially ready, you will have the experience and connections to be successful at it!

Sample Transition Plan:

Here's a template for a six-month plan to transition from your career to your purpose. Since science shows we are more likely to commit to things that we write down, record your goals and progress each month.

Month 1: Research your purpose field, and how you can enter it. Talk to others in the field about how they entered it, and start working more hours or getting an additional job to help prepare your finances for the transition. If friends or family oppose, don't let this deter you and remember it's your life and your purpose.

Month 2: You should be building up your finances and practicing your purpose a bit. Whether through books, videos, research, shadowing, etc., get experience in doing your purpose. For example, if your purpose is motivational speaking, start practicing public speaking by doing Toastmasters, debates, or even recording yourself giving speeches. Develop and hone the skills you'll need for your purpose.

Month 3: By now, you should be building a comfortable financial base, and progressing in your purpose practice. Try doing your purpose on the next level—for example, if you want to be a motivational speaker, start volunteering at local organizations to give speeches to an audience. Build up a resume/portfolio.

Month 4: You should be more than halfway through your transition now. Expand ties in your purpose field, find networking events and start getting into the field.

Month 5: During this month, focus on preparing for a full transition to your purpose. Make sure your finances are comfortable and you have a surefire method of entry into your field.

Month 6: Make the final preparations for your transition. Give notice at your current job and prepare for the new one. Go through job interviews and secure that new purpose!

Soul Work Questions:

1) Are you happy at your current job?

2) How are you going to apply your purpose to help others?

3) How much do you need to save to break free from "corporate" America?

4) Who has done something similar to your purpose that you can learn from?

Purpose Team Project:

Help each other create plans for achieving your purpose, and brainstorm how to put your plans into action.

Chapter 14

Staying Awake

"If we want to stay spiritually awake, we need to seek things that will keep us awake"

Being spiritually awake means we have taken time to forgive everyone, including ourselves. It means we've cleared out the clutter in our system, and now we've made room for God to comfortably reside. When chaos enters our system, we are making God uncomfortable and we need to clear it out as soon as possible. Sometimes chaos enters and it takes over our thoughts, and the next thing we know we are spiritually asleep again. Quick signs of this include weight gain, being moody, watching more TV and reading less, and engaging in gossip and negative behavior. Staying spiritually awake takes work! Because we now take responsibility for our thoughts, we must work at deleting all negative thoughts in our head. It means eating and drinking the way God would have us eat and drink. Many foods block our spiritual third eye and make us sluggish. Eat healthy foods to stay rejuvenated and awake.

If we want to stay spiritually awake, we need to seek things that will keep us awake. One of the daily rituals that I do to stay awake is to go to the mountains for a run and pray each morning. Before I answer emails or have calls, I make sure to do this because I get the energy I need to be successful that day. Many of us may wake up on the "wrong side of the bed" one morning, but after a run and prayer, we are guaranteed to feel amazing! I only want to engage with others in a full and joyous state. Another of my rituals is going every Sunday with my mom and praying, and feeding the birds. This is a reminder to feed those who are less fortunate or perhaps can't feed themselves. I feel a tremendous connection with God being at the ocean. I realize how we are all just a part of a much bigger picture.

As part of this picture, practice forgiving everyone! Not in a few months or a year, but as soon as someone hurts you. That doesn't mean you should let them do it again, but don't hold the resentment or hurt with you. Avoid internal chaos.

Soul Work Questions:

1) What do you do to stay spiritually awake?

2) Do you take time to pray and meditate each day?

3) Do you surround yourself with other people who are awake?

4) What are some things you can do to build your Spirituality muscle?

Purpose Team Project:

Take time to pray and meditate together. To meditate, simply set aside some quiet time to self-reflect and look into yourself for guidance. A good place to go would be a shrine or temple, and if you live near or visit Los Angeles, the Shrine in Pacific Palisades is a perfect place to meditate. Reflect on your shared bond and spirituality and help each other advance.

Chapter 15

Learn How To Speak to God

"Know how God speaks and look for signs"

When I was 7 years old, my uncle taught me how to speak to God. He taught whenever I wanted to communicate, be quiet and simply ask God what I wanted to know. God would answer me. At first, it was hard to be in a room without noise and without getting the urge to talk, but pretty soon I was able to speak to God.

When I was 14, I got angry at God and said I never wanted to hear from God again because I was hurt and felt the life I had was unfair. Later of course, I found God gave me this life with purpose, but in that moment, I didn't want to hear anything about God. The next few years were terrible. It wasn't until I realized it wasn't God's fault, that I started to speak with God again. It felt amazing! Life became a lot easier, and now I work hard to stay awake so that I can hear God.

God can speak to us in many different ways. God's voice can be your child giving you a message or God can speak to you in dreams or through intuition. Many of us have missed God's messages because we didn't know it was God speaking.

A great example is: I was at a meeting the other day with a Hollywood director. I've been debating a certain issue, and she gave me the advice I needed exactly at the right time. I knew in that moment it was God speaking through her. She didn't realize it, but I sure did. When that happens, I usually get chills on my arms. It's a wonderful experience to be able to recognize God's energy in others. When God is trying to get a message to us and we are not seeing the signs, God will start to get louder with bolder messages. For example, if God wants you to redirect your life and you are not listening, you may find yourself sick and now you really have to think about it. That's why so many people, after surviving sickness, change their careers. For the first time, they had time to be in silence and with God to get direction. We've got to learn to be quiet and still if we really want to hear God.

I didn't hear God for 14 years of my life and it was one of

the loneliest and darkest times of my life. I thought everything rested on me and not on God's plan. I wanted to control everything, because I didn't know God had a plan for me.

Know how God speaks and look for signs. It comes slow, and then it overwhelms you. If you are not able to communicate with God go to these places and be in silence:

- The beach

- Gardens

- The Mountains

- Rivers

Frequency has everything to do with your ability to speak with God. Lower frequency places: it's harder to communicate but it's still possible. Higher frequency places: it's very easy and you will feel like you never want to leave those places.

God never stops talking—we stop listening. We all have the ability to hear God but we've got to work at it! The first thing we've got to do is clear out our internal chaos and we've got to still the mind. Then we've got to go somewhere in nature and be still. God will begin speaking and pretty soon you will be in constant communication, not because you *have* to, but because you *want* to.

Soul Work:

1) Where are some places you can go to hear God?

2) What are times God might have spoken to you, but you ignored the signs? Learn to recognize these signs so you can look out for them next time!

3) What is something you want to tell God? Tell him!

Purpose Team Project:

Go to a place where you can hear God. Pray together, meditate, self-reflect—privately. Talk to God for guidance, and share any good advice he has!

Chapter 16

The Basics

"Success is always right around the corner if you just keep

trying."

Making Mistakes

In today's society, we are taught to strive for perfection but the

reality is we're all going to make mistakes along the way and

that's okay! The important thing is to deal with mistakes in a

healthy and positive way. When dealing with mistakes, most

punish themselves in some form. Either they quit on a project or

resort to pleasures like food, alcohol, sex, drugs to numb the pain.

That's only temporary relief and the pain/guilt eventually returns.

We need to learn to deal with mistakes in a much healthier way.

Here are a few tips you can use the next time you make a

mistake:

- Know you are human and making mistakes is inevitable.

- Analyze your mistake and work hard at not repeating the mistake.

- LET IT GO and work on doing better in the future.

Never Giving Up

Thomas Edison had to try over 1,000 times to invent the light bulb. Had he given up, we would have never been gifted with light. Some people would have given up after ten tries and thought they failed, but not Mr. Edison. He was determined to make it work and because of his perseverance millions of people benefited. The next time you are working on a new business, new dream, and new project, don't give up the first time you encounter an obstacle. Keep going and never give up! Success is always right around the corner if you just persevere.

Here are a few tips you can use the next time you feel like giving up:

- Stay positive throughout the day by saying positive affirmations like: "With God all things are possible."

- Think of new ways you can make your project/dream possible.

- Contact possible mentors who can help you get through hard times.

Passing of A Friend/Family Member

Please know in your heart that it was their time to go. This is when they wrote it in their blueprint. Mourn for a season and then pick yourself back up and find comfort in knowing they never left your side. We are all energy and if you ever want to speak to them know you can. Our friends and loved ones on the other side are always trying to communicate with us. Sometimes just to say hello or to give us a message.

For instance, a good friend of mine who is a big time DJ believes that his late father, who was a minister, tries to communicate with him when he sees dimes that are faced up. He says he will see it especially when he is having a bad day and that it his dad's way of saying he is with him. My grandmother comes to me as a white butterfly. I see her whenever I'm nervous before a big meeting. She had tons of confidence, so when I see the butterfly I am filled with her courage.

How to Know If A Person Should Be In Your Life

Not everyone is intended to be in our lives for our "entire book," but rather just for a chapter or two. The best way to know if their season is up is if they begin to disrespect you. Anyone who truly loves you will never say or do anything to hurt you. Our energy is something we have to protect because we need to be able to communicate with God. When we are filled with negativity it is impossible to be a vessel for God. I ask myself, *"Is this person going to get me off track on my purpose?"* and *"Does this person mean well for me?"* Don't be afraid to just stop hanging out with certain people for your good!

How To Know What To Do With a Job Situation

You will know in your heart if you should leave a job or not. Pray and get in your Higher Self state and ask God. Be still and the answer will come to you either internally or via a sign. Being still means being in a space to receive the message where you can hear God.

Example of being still and being able to receive God's message:

Prayer → Beach/Meditation → Answer

Example of NOT being still and NOT being able to receive God's message:

Prayer → Vegas/ Club Arguments → NO Answer

Focus On The Right Things

It can be easy to focus on an obstacle, and before you know it, you are attracting more bad stuff to your life. The reality is when we think negative, negative things happen in our life. We need to learn how to redirect our focus. A great example is when someone has a breakup with their partner, their work is usually affected and they are either let go, or if they own the business, they see a loss because their focus is not there. We need to learn to redirect our focus to positive thoughts versus negative thoughts. We will always have obstacles in our life but I believe they are in our lives so we can learn from them, not so they can harm us.

Here are a few tips you can use the next time you are feeling negative/down:

- Think of all of the great things in your life you are grateful for like your health, family, car, job, etc.

- Know that negative thoughts don't last forever. Take a break and think of a positive thought.

- Every minute we have over 48 thoughts. Learn to select the positive ones and focus on those.

Be Patient When We Are Being Redirected

We are going to be rejected many times during our lives. Instead of taking it personally, realize you are simply being redirected to something better. For example, if you are fired, then God is redirecting you to a better opportunity. You're either going to get a better job or you are going to start a new business or you're finally going to pursue your purpose. If God is taking a relationship away from you, it's because the universe has someone better for you. We need to trust that nothing is done to hurt us, but simply to redirect us.

Here are a few tips you can use the next time you are being redirected:

- Being redirected is painful because you are losing something. This is your time to get closer to God and trust something better is on its way.

- Don't make it personal. Nothing we have done in life is in vain.

- Realize there are seasons for everything. Some jobs/people are not meant to be in our life an entire lifetime, maybe just a few seasons.

Perseverance

I worked for a millionaire when I was young. He was fired from his job, and I learned a valuable lesson through his journey. Nothing is forever. Bad times or good times. What matters most is: are you willing to get back up and try and again and again until you make it work? That boss ended up getting a bigger opportunity that quadrupled his income within months. Had he lost hope and given up he would have never received that blessing. If you are having bad times, know that good times are coming, but you must get up and give it all you got!

Here are a few tips you can use the next time you're going through a hard time:

- Know that it will not last forever! We all have bad seasons and this is yours. Plant seeds so next season you will have an abundance.

- When you are having good times save/plan/give/reinvest so that you no longer have bad seasons.

- This is your time to get closer to God and ask what He would have you do. Follow that. Doing God's work will bring you the greatest success!

Stay On Track

So many people are worried about the wrong things nowadays. We all need to be reminded that our focus should be on our dreams. When I used to work in corporate America, I would see zombies in the office who never moved up but were just content with their salary and did just enough to get by. Their energy was negative and they never had anything good to say. I did my best to stay away from those people and I just went to work and did what I had to do and left.

Because of my philosophy I was the youngest person to resign, since I started my own company that turned into the #1 publicity company in Hollywood. Don't get too comfortable, go and get what you came here for!

Here are a few tips you can use the next time you feel stagnant:

- Ask yourself what more you can be doing to realize your dreams.

- Who in your circle needs to go because you can no longer tolerate people who are negative or gossipers.

- Keep a weekly to do list of what you need to achieve and make sure you cross everything off by Friday.

Follow Your Heart

Many parents want their children to become doctors or lawyers because they want to see them succeed, but that ultimately slows their children from pursuing their true calling. Parental pressure is one of the hardest to overcome to do what our heart says to be right. I encourage each and every one of you to listen to your heart. The great thing about following your heart is God opens doors for you and you become more successful than a doctor/lawyer could ever dream. We have to stop listening to outside sources and we need to trust our heart.

Here are a few tips you can use the next time you are going to make a big decision and you want to follow your heart:

- Ask God, "Lord I'm about to make _____ decision is it the right move to make?" Stay quiet and the answer will come to you.
- Ask yourself, "Is this going to benefit just me or others as well?" If it's just to benefit you, odds are you are making decisions based on your brain and not your heart

Don't Pay Attention to Haters

The only person who can determine how successful we can be is ourselves. When I was in high school, my counselor told me I wasn't USC material. Sadly, I believed her and didn't apply for admission, even though I had a 4.2 GPA, was the best all-round volleyball player, and held a full-time job. Little by little, I built my confidence back and I earned straight A's at Mt. San Antonio

College. Two years later, I was admitted to USC. I could have graduated early, but decided to take on another major so I could graduate with my class. Now I mentor USC students, I speak at their events and my book is sold in the Trojan bookstore. So turns out I AM USC material—my high school counselor just couldn't or wouldn't see it. We can never let other people's opinion of us define who we are!

Here are a few tips you can use the next time someone tells you something negative about your life/journey/plan:

- Remember their opinion of you or your dream does not matter

- Share your passion/purpose with those who are also pursuing theirs. Otherwise you are sure to come across conflict because others will simply not understand and will try and sabotage you/send negativity your way.

- Realize that God's plan for you is beyond anyone's beliefs…sometimes it can be hard to believe it but when we trust God we know that all things are possible. Even this biggest dream can be achieved when we do it for God.

Getting Started

Many people think that they don't have what it takes to start their calling/new business/purpose/foundation but the reality is, we all have exactly what we need to make our dream a reality. The important part is to START. Begin where you are and with what you have, and things will work themselves out as you go along. Napoleon Hill says 98-100 percent of people never have the courage to chase their dreams because they lack faith. Be part of the 2 percent that DOES have faith and goes after their dreams with passion!

Here are a few tips you can use the next time you want to start but feel fear and retreat:

- Know that if God put an idea in your heart it's because you will be successful at it.

- Everyone encounters obstacles. Don't let them stop you. Learn how to make them work for you.

- Work on a positive mind. When you are pursuing your purpose the smallest amount of doubt will ruin the plan. Focus the mind on prayer and God will do the rest.

Pursuing Your Purpose in Life

Above all, love yourself, respect yourself, and have patience with yourself. So many times we lose these three simple things because deep down many people feel unworthy. We need to realize that we are worthy and all deserve happiness. The best way to achieve that is by putting our self first and by being true to who we are, versus who others want us to be.

Let's say you are a musician at heart, but you feel pressure to have a 9-5 job to be "normal." It doesn't matter what *job* you have, you will be miserable because your heart wants to "be in music". We need to do what our heart desires and be true to our gift so that God can abundantly bless us.

Soul Work:

Ask Yourself

- Who am I living this life for?

- Am I doing what my heart desires?

- When I die will I be content with what I have done here?

Purpose Team Project:

Share your answers to the soul work questions with your purpose people. Reflect on what you have learned throughout the book, and write down ways you will continue meeting and growing with your purpose people, using this book as a launch pad and blueprint. This book is only the beginning of your success and your journey to discover your purpose. I wish you the best of luck!

Final Thoughts

Finding your purpose is the most important thing you can do in your life. It's not graduating high school or getting into the best college or even getting married. Being awakened and pursuing your purpose is the most important! This life is temporary but heaven is forever. It's important that we do what we were sent to do.

It's because I found my purpose that my life has transformed and I no longer fear obstacles or death! The only thing I fear is being disobedient to God. I know when I leave here I'm going right back to where we all go and we're once again reunited with our creator. I want God to know I gave it my all to awaken, to uplift, to inspire, motivate and most importantly love my brothers and sisters.

Acknowledgments

I want to thank God for guiding me! I want to thank my parents for loving me and allowing me to fully pursue my purpose with their support. They are my rock and best friends.

I want to thank Andrew Corona for being there every step of the way during my awakening. This book would not have been possible without his support!

I'd like to honor and thank Nicolas Blass Brunet. He taught me it was "ok" to live a life of service to others and to be a proud servant of God. He taught me many lessons; the greatest of which was to be who God intended me to be versus who society wants me to be.

I'd like to thank Madelyn Chen for helping relieve my work burdens and going above and beyond to succeed on the tasks I gave her. Thank you for helping me with this book, and here's to our continued work and success together.

I'd like to thank Michael Smith from Covington Capital Management for being a great friend and for believing in me!

I'd like to thank Darrin Cook for turning my vision in

reality, you are amazing at what you do!

I want to thank all of my mentors for teaching me lessons that are not in books and for opening doors I didn't even know existed! I'm humbled by your kindness and love.

I want to thank all of my friends. I've learned and grown because I've had the ability to spend time with you. Thank you for wisdom, love and care! You're all in my heart always.

Elvira Guzman Biography

Elvira Guzman, a Southern California native, owns one of the fastest growing PR & Branding companies in Hollywood, CA. Ms. Guzman was recognized by Success Magazine and Black Enterprise Magazine. Prior to her independent success she worked for Steve Harvey for 9 years. Not only was she featured in Latina Magazine's September issue and is considered one of "The Future 15 Latino Entrepreneurs". From her life experiences she was able to compile her life lessons into a book that can help improve the lives of others, called *Your Blueprint*, along with this book, *Purpose*. Ms. Guzman has created seminars to empower others both in the US and abroad. Additionally, in the states, Ms. Guzman lends her time to speak at juvenile halls, at-risk high schools, universities, and organizations.

45089236R00095

Made in the USA
San Bernardino, CA
02 February 2017